CW01022492

illustrated by : Jade Mempin

Table of Contents

Introduction

Hello, extraordinary girl!

In these stories, you'll meet regular girls who faced challenges just like you. They didn't have superpowers or fancy gadgets, but they had something even more important: courage.

Life can throw curveballs, and sometimes you might doubt yourself. It happens to the best of us. But what you're about to discover in these stories is that doubt can be defeated, fears can be conquered, and dreams can become your reality.

Here's the secret: You're never alone in this journey called life. The characters in these stories, and so many others out there, have walked a similar path.

They've faced struggles, climbed mountains, and turned their dreams into accomplishments. Now, it's your turn. These stories are like roadmaps, guiding you on a journey of self-discovery, self-confidence, and unwavering self-esteem.

Believe in yourself, just as we believe in you. You've got what it takes to tackle any challenge, bounce back from setbacks, and achieve greatness. You're more extraordinary than you know.

So, as you flip through these pages and dive into the first story, remember this: Your journey to becoming the hero of your own inspiring story starts right here, right now. You're ready. Your time is here. Let's begin this incredible adventure together!

Lisa and The Bully

Have you ever met a bully? Maybe someone has picked on you, or on someone you care about - or maybe on someone you didn't even know. Did it make you feel uncomfortable? Were you afraid to stand up for yourself?

Let me tell you a story about a girl called Lisa. Something like this happened to her.

Lisa was in school, like every other day. She was in the yard, passing a ball around with two of her classmates, Hayley and Gail. They were waiting for the bell to ring them in for history class with Miss Whitman.

A few paces away stood Zoey by herself. She looked a bit nervous, and kept looking up at the time.

"Should we ask Zoey if she wants to come kick some ball before we go in?" Lisa asked Hayley. "She looks a bit sad."

But, Hayley didn't have time to answer, and Lisa didn't have time to ask. Before they knew it, Veronica came out from behind the corner of the school building. Zoey turned pale. Veronica was big, and strong, and a year older than them, and she was walking right for Zoey.

"Hey!"

Zoey tried to ignore her. Veronica walked right up to her and pushed her on the shoulder.

"I said 'Hey'. I'm talking to you! Don't you answer when people talk? What's the matter, can't you talk? Are you a little baby?"

Lisa wanted to say something. She wanted to help Zoey. She wanted to do something! But she didn't say anything. It felt like her arms and her stomach were ice cold, and a hard lump was forming in her throat.

Zoey just stood there and helplessly said, "Leave me alone, Veronica, it's not funny…"

Lisa looked over at Hayley and Gail to see if they would come with her, but they were kicking the ball, looking down.

Veronica kept pushing Zoey.

"Well, I think it's funny!" she said. Then, she took Zoey's hair bobbin and threw it on the ground. "Oh no, the little baby lost her baby-bobbin! Better pick it up before someone steps on it."

Zoey went to pick it up, but Veronica stuck her dirty shoe in and stepped right on it. The Ice inside Lisa started moving. She wanted so badly to go up and tell Veronica to stop, it just didn't happen. Then, thankfully, Miss Whitman came out through the door.

"Is everything okay?" she asked and looked around.

Zoey said nothing. Lisa said nothing. Hayley and Gail stopped kicking their ball, but they said nothing. Veronica took a step to the side.

"We were just playing", she said innocently.

Miss Whitman looked down at Zoey. "Is that true?"

Zoey nodded quietly. The bell rang, and everyone went back inside.

Lisa was thinking about it all day. She was sad for Zoey. She was angry with Veronica, but she was even more angry with herself. How could she just stand there? How could she be so afraid? None of her friends had done anything either. They must have been scared, too.

She didn't walk home with Hayley as usual. She walked by herself, the long way home. Slowly, she dragged her feet forwards, thinking through the ache between her stomach and her chest. Maybe she could talk to Zoey? But what could she say? No, she felt ashamed to say anything when she didn't do anything.

When she came home, her big brother was in the front yard, messing with his moped. She felt a bit hopeful. Maybe he could help, he was the bravest person she knew.

"Who peed in your Cornflakes?" he asked when he saw how sad she looked.

"Ha-ha..." Lisa rolled her eyes. Then, she stood there for a while, thinking if she should say something. "Hey, Colin, can I ask you something? What do you do when you're scared?"

Colin looked up. "Scared? Who are you scared of? You want me to beat him up?"

Lisa shook her head. "There's this girl..."

Now, Colin shook his head. "Ah, well in that case, no can do - you'll have to do it yourself!"

Lisa started to get a bit annoyed. "Stop joking, I'm serious! Something happened today, and this bigger girl was mean to one of my friends, and..."

Colin took on a more brotherly look.

"What happened? What did you do?"

"Nothing, alright? That's the problem. I did nothing to help my friend. Do you think… If you're scared to do something that's right, does that mean you're going to be a coward forever?"

Colin made big eyes at her. "Of course not! Everything that's worth doing is hard and scary. That's how you know it's the right thing. That's why they call bad things like lying and looking the other way 'the easy way out'. You're not a coward for being scared." He then put his arm around her. "It is important to do the right thing, though, especially when you're scared. I'm sure this bully doesn't know what she has coming the next time she runs into you. Don't beat anyone up, but don't walk away either. You'll learn where there's balance. Okay?"

Lisa thought about their talk all afternoon. Somehow, it made sense. She wasn't going to be afraid anymore.

The next day in school, Lisa felt different. Just before lunch, Veronica walked towards Zoey again, with a mean grin on her face.

"Hey, crybaby, give me your lunch money!"

Lisa felt her heart race and arms go cold, but this time, she didn't just stand there. Veronica walked up and pushed Zoey on the shoulder, but Lisa's legs didn't freeze. Instead they started moving, and didn't stop until she was standing between Zoey and Veronica.

"Stop pushing my friend!" she said, way louder than she thought she would. Veronica frowned.

"Don't get involved, it's none of your business!"

Lisa swallowed hard. "Yes, it is. Don't push my friend!"

Veronica looked angry.

"Okay, suit yourself!"

Lisa didn't expect it, but Veronica hit her, in the eye. It was very sore, but Lisa didn't move.

Miss Whitman came running out.

"What is going on out here? I saw that from the window, young lady! You're both going to get a talking to and I'm ringing both your parents, but I'm going to start with you, Veronica, because that is not okay!"

When Lisa turned around, Zoey jumped at her and hugged her super hard.

"Thank you! She's been mean to me all year! I'm sorry she hit you, are you okay?"

Lisa smiled. Sure - her eye hurt... but it hurt way less than her stomach had from not doing the right thing.

See, when we do scary things because our conscience tells us to, it makes us brave. All it takes for you to be brave, is not to look away when something bad happens. If everyone had each other's backs like Lisa did Zoey's, the world would be a better, braver place.

Carrie's New Phone

Have you ever felt a little sad when you got a present because it wasn't exactly like a gift someone else got? That feeling is called envy, and it happens to a lot of people sometimes.

Our next story is about Carrie, and she went through this, right on her birthday.

Carrie's friend Chloe had received a super cool, brand new phone for her birthday. It was big, bright, loud, and could do all sorts of fun things with fancy apps. Chloe could take pictures with cool effects, filters, and add captions too!

Carrie knew her birthday was coming up, so she asked her mom if she could have a new phone.

"A new phone?" Mom pondered. "Well, you've been doing such a great job with your chores and homework lately. Let's see what we can do, alright?"

Carrie's family didn't have lots of money to spend on fancy stuff, but they always made sure Carrie had a wonderful birthday. Her mom baked a scrumptious cake with layers of fruit and jam, dad came home early from work, they sang songs, and she even had a small party on the closest Friday. She always wished for big, floating balloons, but usually, they were the regular ones her mom had to blow up herself. When she asked her parents, they replied just like always.

Mom would say, "Those big balloons always fly away. Why get ones that disappear in five minutes?"

Dad would say, "I'm not made of helium! The regular ones come in big packs!"

That was that, Mom and Dad had the final say.

This year, Carrie's birthday happened to fall on a Friday, so she could have her party on her actual birthday. Carrie was excited. She roamed around all day, avoiding her busy mom who was cleaning the whole apartment. Carrie didn't quite understand why her mom was cleaning so much, knowing they would make a big mess soon while baking, setting up, and playing. Besides, it would look even messier after her friends arrived. Dad had worked extra hours that week, so he came home early at one o'clock to buy party supplies and candies for the cake.

For some reason, Carrie felt a little nervous about her birthday this year. It was usually all about fun – baking, helping with balloons, playing with friends, and opening presents.

But this year, her worries about the phone made her think about other things that weren't going as she wanted.

She was so nervous about what her friends would think of her party that she couldn't enjoy their company when they came knocking at the door. Chloe arrived first, as usual, looking super happy and excited, with a nicely wrapped present in hand.

"Hey, I want to take a photo of you with the cake using my new phone! I can add cool effects like a moving party hat and a gazillion balloons!" Chloe said as she scrolled through her phone's cool features. "Did your mom bake this cake herself?" she asked. "It's covered in so many colorful sprinkles!"

"Oh, Carrie helped a lot!" Mom replied. "She's excellent at mixing and cracking eggs!"

Carrie blushed again.

Throughout the day, her worries continued. While playing a game called fishpond, she couldn't help but notice that Chloe had six sweets and a toy in each bag while she had fewer sweets.

When it was time for "Pin The Tail on The Donkey," all she could think about was how at Chloe's party, they had a real-looking donkey picture, while hers was just a silly drawing her dad had made with its tongue sticking out.

Afterward, they enjoyed cake, and it was finally time to open the presents. Carrie carefully unwrapped each one, saving the gift from her mom and dad for last. Chloe had gifted her some lovely unicorn-shaped erasers and colorful pencils, Loretta had given her a beautiful coloring book, and Fiona had given her a cute, fluffy sheep with a "Friends Forever" collar.

The present from her mom and dad was a small, rectangular box that looked like it could be a phone! She opened it carefully... It was a phone!

But it was smaller and not new at all.

"It has some scratches on the back," she sadly remarked.

Mom tried to make her feel better.

"Well, just a few, because it's a second-hand one... but it's still good! The salesman assured us that it's in perfect working condition. You can still use some apps and text your friends, you know?"

Carrie felt a mix of emotions building up inside her. Her birthday happiness turned into tears, and she started saying things she didn't mean.

"But... I wanted a nice phone! A new one, like what everyone else has!" She sniffled. "And I wanted a cake that looks amazing, like Chloe's! I wanted those floating balloons that stay up, not the plain ones from the store! And I wanted a realistic donkey for the game, and the fishpond sheet to have fish and more surprises in the bags!"

Carrie was crying, and her friends fell silent. Mom looked sad, and dad seemed a bit frustrated.

"Carrie, that's not the way to talk to your mom! She's been working hard since early morning to make your birthday special! What you said was unkind and ungrateful, young lady. I'm half-tempted to send your friends home right now."

Carrie continued crying. "That's okay, because they probably can't wait to leave this boring party!"

She ran outside and sat alone in the garden, like she often did when feeling very sad. Everything seemed disappointing. She was afraid to go back inside because her parents would be upset, and her friends probably thought her party was dull. Everything seemed bad for her, while it looked perfect for everyone else.

Suddenly, she heard a noise and jumped. Chloe was standing right behind her.

"Hey, are you okay?" Chloe asked as she sat down beside her.

"I'm okay," Carrie sniffled. "I just had the worst birthday party ever because my life is not fun."

"Your life isn't not fun!" Chloe reassured her. "Come on..." Chloe put her arm around Carrie and gave her a comforting hug. "I don't think it's the worst birthday party ever."

Carrie shrugged. "You're just saying that to be nice."

Chloe hugged her even tighter. "No, I'm not! Do you want to know something? My mom never lets me help bake anything. I've never even seen her bake before! She says it makes too much of a mess in the kitchen. I get a nice cake from the bakery, but I don't get to bake. In your house, everyone can play as much as they want without anyone telling you to 'stop making a mess.' You want to know something else? My dad buys me lots of presents, but he's never come home early to celebrate my birthday with me. He's never home early at all. Your dad drew a funny donkey for you that looks like it's having fun with the game! You know that big picture of a regular donkey? It doesn't even look bothered by having a tail pinned to it!"

They both chuckled.

"It's all different," Chloe said. "I'm happy I got my phone, a big party, and a pretty cake, but you should be happy that your family wants to be with you on your birthday."

Carrie wiped her tears away, feeling a bit silly.

"I'm sorry," she said. "Thank you... I'm going to apologize to my mom now. I hope she's not too upset."

Chloe gave her one last hug. "You know why I always want to be here when we're playing? Because your family is so nice."

Carrie almost started crying again.

"You can be here as much as you want," she said, and they both went back inside.

You see, Carrie thought everything was bad because she didn't get exactly what her friends got. It's a tricky feeling, for sure. But sometimes, it's important to remember that everyone has different good things and different challenges. Sometimes, it's good to appreciate what you have and not just focus on what you don't. Carrie might not have the fanciest phone in school, but she has something even better - a loving family and a wonderful friend like Chloe.

Daisy and The Turning Point

Have you ever faced the challenge of peer pressure, where friends push you into something that doesn't sit right with your values? It's a common part of growing up, and it's important to distinguish between harmless fun and actions that are genuinely harmful or wrong.

Daisy was known as a good girl, well, most of the time. She held herself to high standards, refraining from using inappropriate language around adults, never cheating on tests, and never engaging in activities that might weigh on her conscience. Her dad always emphasized, "A clear conscience is the best pillow," and she took his words to heart.

Daisy cherished her friendships with Sarah and Emily. They were kind-hearted and beautiful, though not as academically inclined as she and her other close friend, Julia. Daisy and Julia often helped Sarah and Emily with their studies, from math to essay writing. Occasionally, Sarah and Emily groaned about the workload but benefited from their assistance.

When all four friends were together, it was easier for Daisy to decline certain requests. Julia was known for her independence and would speak her mind even to adults. "No," she'd say firmly, "you won't learn anything if we just do it for you." Daisy backed her up, saying, "If the teacher asks you a question

about it in class, you won't know what to say."
Julia added, "Besides, none of you have my
handwriting, and you don't spell as well as we
do."

However, on days when Julia had other
commitments, like track practice or field
hockey, it was just Daisy, Sarah, and Emily. It
became harder for her to resist peer pressure
when they joined forces.

"You know we're never gonna remember any
of this anyway, right?" Sarah would say, with
Emily nodding in agreement. "We don't want to
be accountants or bankers. I'm gonna be an
influencer, and they don't need to do math."

"I'm sure they have to sometimes…" Daisy
replied, but her friends mocked her, making
her feel embarrassed for caring about
schoolwork. She didn't want to be seen as
boring, so sometimes she reluctantly gave in.

One Friday, after school, Emily was excited
about her good grades. "Thanks to Daisy," she
said, "I get to have a sleepover."

Daisy felt both proud and ashamed, but Emily reassured her, "Daisy made us study so hard for this, and we did really well."

Julia, who had track practice that evening, couldn't join the sleepover. Emily welcomed Sarah and Daisy to her house, and they prepared for a fun night.

Emily, alone in the kitchen, pulled out snacks and soda. "My mom's not home. She's with her boyfriend. I'm supposed to be at my dad's, but he doesn't really know that."

Daisy felt uneasy. "Aren't you worried about being alone without your parents knowing where you are?"

Emily laughed it off, "We're not babies, we don't need someone watching us all the time. If it makes you feel better, we all know how to dial 911. Now, let's make popcorn and enjoy some soda!"

Initially, everything was fine. They laughed, ate snacks, watched movies, and talked about various topics, including boys. They were having a great time, making goofy faces and sending playful texts.

Then, Sarah suggested playing Truth or Dare.

At first, the dares were harmless, but then Emily disappeared briefly and returned with a pack of cigarettes. "I dare you to smoke one of these," she said, laughing.

Daisy's heart sank, but she hesitated, torn between her desire to fit in and her principles. She reluctantly took the cigarette, but before she could light it, Julia stormed in.

"Are you out of your minds? Smoking indoors? Your mom is going to be furious, Emily!"

Julia scolded them, especially Daisy. Daisy, on the verge of tears, agreed that it was a terrible idea. Julia explained, "You have to stand up for yourself; otherwise, they'll keep pressuring you into doing things you don't want to do. Real friends wouldn't do that."

Emily defended her actions, saying they invited Daisy because she was "lame" and did their homework. Julia had a different perspective, though. "I can't be around bad influences; it'll ruin my sports dreams. You know what I can be around? Lame people who behave and do well in school."

Daisy left with Julia, and the two had a sleepover at Julia's house. On the way, Daisy apologized for her actions, but Julia reminded her to apologize to herself and learn to stand up for what she believed in.

Peer pressure can sway us in various directions, but it's crucial to think about the consequences and remain true to our values. Ultimately, no one can dictate our choices if we assert ourselves and surround ourselves with friends who respect us for who we are.

Lisa and The Bully Pt.2
Veronica's Conscience

Remember Lisa, and when she got punched in the face by a bully? It's easy to think of bullies as these horrible monster-people who want to hurt everyone, but sometimes, the story doesn't end there. People who feel bad, hurt other people, because they don't know how to feel better.

Remember Veronica, who was being mean to Zoey, pushing her around, stepping on her bobbin and taking her lunch money? This is what happened afterwards.

It had been a few weeks and Veronica hadn't been mean to Zoey at all. Zoey and Lisa were very good friends nowadays and were hanging out after school a lot. Zoey was very shy and quiet, but she was a lot happier now that she wasn't being picked on and got to eat her lunch every day. Lisa and Zoey even walked home almost every day.

One day, however, Zoey was going to the dentist with her mom, and Lisa, who felt a lot more brave these days, thought she might take a little stroll before going home. She walked around for a while until she saw that she was close to a little path going into a patch of woods. It wasn't like a real, big forest, but it had one of those running trails and there were a lot of birds.

Lisa skipped along the trail, hopping over tree roots and stones, listening to the chittering and chattering in the canopy... and then, she heard a noise. It sounded like someone crying.

Along the trail, there were benches in certain places. On one of those benches, Veronica was sitting, crying into her hands. Lisa stopped. What was she supposed to do? She could turn around and go back without saying anything. It was Veronica - she was mean all the time!

Lisa could have walked away.

Lisa could have said something mean now that Veronica was the one who was sad.

But Lisa thought about what her brother had said about being brave. "That's why they call lying and looking the other way 'the easy way out'."

Lisa walked up to Veronica. Veronica didn't see her at first, she was only sitting there, crying.

"Hi", Lisa said. "Why are you so sad?"

Veronica was startled and jumped back. "What? Oh, it's you… What do you want?" she snarled.

"Why are you crying?" Lisa persisted.

"What's it to you?" mumbled Veronica.

Lisa's heart was thumping loudly in her chest. She was afraid that keeping this up would get her another sock in the eye. She was worried Veronica would say mean things or threaten her. She stayed, though, and she kept calm.

"Nothing, but… You know what? My mom taught me that you should never ignore someone who's in pain. You're crying. If you want to talk about why you're sad… You can talk to me, okay?"

Veronica looked up and tried to put on an indifferent face, maybe look threatening, but she couldn't stop crying. The tears were falling out like raindrops on a freckled pavement.

"What, so you can laugh at me and tell everyone at school?"

Lisa shook her head. "I wouldn't do that. I'm not like that."

For whatever reason, it seemed like Veronica was about to give up. She was already crying in front of someone else and nothing was going to make her feel better if she started a fight. Maybe it was because Lisa was being genuinely kind.

"It's… my dad, okay? My dad is moving away from our house. He's going to live somewhere else, and my parents are getting a divorce."

She cried even harder and hid her face in her hands. Lisa sat down next to her.

"That's so sad… I'm sorry your parents are fighting…"

"They were fighting when we were in the first grade, too", Veronica sniffled, "And I asked them if they were going to get a divorce, and my mom said, 'No, dad and I are never going to move apart'… and they were just lying!"

Veronica cried so much, her shirt sleeve was getting soaked. Lisa put her arm around Veronica.

"I'm sorry that's happening", Lisa said. "Is your dad moving very far away?"

"He's moving somewhere else where he got a job and an apartment or something… I'm gonna live with my mom, and he's gonna be all gone. When they're fighting, my mom says it won't even make a difference that he's not there because he's always out anyway, but it will make a difference for me!"

Veronica could barely speak anymore, and neither could Lisa. It was all so sad. Lisa didn't know what to say, but maybe it would be best not to talk anyway. What could she say? She sat there, with her arm around Veronica, who kept crying.

"Can I ask you something?" Lisa finally said. "Why do you keep teasing and pushing people?"

"I don't know", Veronica cried. "I'm just angry all the time and nobody cares about me anyway, so why should I care about them?"

Lisa took a deep breath.

"But I care."

Veronica looked up. At first, she looked angry again, like she was thinking about taking it all back and running away, but then she leaned over onto Lisa's shoulder and wept quietly.

"A lot of people would care that you're sad", Lisa sniffled. "Don't be mean, be… Be our friend instead, okay?"

Veronica didn't even look up. "No one will want to be friends with me anymore, you're just saying that because I'm crying."

Lisa hugged Veronica harder. "I'm not lying. You'll see. And even if you don't want to talk to anyone else, you can still talk to me whenever you want." She took up her phone. "You can have my phone number and we can always talk."

From that day on, Veronica was a lot nicer to people. Sometimes, she felt angry and sad and alone, but at least she had a friend. Lisa was

happy that things were better now, and invited
Veronica along for all kinds of things.

You see, some people don't know how to tell
others that they're not feeling okay, and they
can lash out, like Veronica did. In a lot of cases,
all they need is for someone to listen to them.
You should never let anyone keep hurting you
or be mean to you just because they're sad –
that's different and you should ask someone
for help if that's happening to you – but if
someone genuinely needs your understanding
and shows that they're actually different, the
kind thing to do, is to at least give them a fair
chance.

Hey There

Thank you for reaching this point in the book!

I thoroughly enjoyed writing this chapter and sincerely hope you found it beneficial. If you have a moment, I would greatly appreciate hearing your thoughts on how you've enjoyed the book thus far.

Your honest feedback means the world to me and is invaluable in helping me improve my future content and create the best resources possible.

You can share your thoughts by visiting the following link or scanning the provided QR code.

SCAN THE QR CODE OR VISIT:

www.bit.ly/inspiringirl

Thank you for taking the time to leave your feedback. Now let's get back into the book.

The Little Shy Writer

Mia was an extraordinary young girl. At just eleven years old, she possessed a remarkable talent that set her apart from her peers–she was a gifted writer. Her vivid imagination and way with words allowed her to craft captivating stories that transported readers to far-off lands, introduced them to intriguing characters, and left them with profound emotions. Mia's creativity knew no bounds, and her stories flowed effortlessly from her heart to the pages of her notebook.

One sunny afternoon, as she sat by her bedroom window with her notebook in hand, Mia decided to enter a local literary contest. She had been encouraged by her parents and teachers for years, but the prospect of submitting her work for judgment had always made her nervous. However, something inside her urged her to take that leap of faith and share her talent with the world.

Weeks of late-night writing sessions followed. Mia poured her soul into a short story that she believed captured the essence of her creativity. It was a tale of an adventurous young girl who discovered a hidden world in her grandmother's attic, complete with enchanted objects and talking animals. The story was a masterpiece, a testament to Mia's boundless imagination and skillful storytelling.

When the day came to submit her entry, Mia hesitated for a moment before clicking the "Submit" button on the contest's website. The feeling of vulnerability washed over her like a tidal wave, but she held her ground. She knew that the only way to grow as a writer was to face her fears and put her work out into the world.

Weeks turned into months, and Mia almost forgot about the contest amidst her everyday life of school, homework, and family dinners. Then, one evening, her father rushed into her room, his face beaming with pride. "Mia, you won!" he exclaimed, holding up his phone to show her the email notification. Mia's heart skipped a beat as she read the words on the screen: "Congratulations, Mia! You have won first place in our literary contest!"

Tears of joy filled her eyes as she hugged her father tightly. She couldn't believe it. Her story had resonated with the judges, and they had recognized her talent. The local literary society was going to hold a special awards ceremony to honor the winners, and Mia was to be the guest of honor.

The days leading up to the ceremony were a whirlwind of excitement and anxiety for Mia. The thought of speaking in front of a large audience terrified her. She was known for her shyness, and the idea of standing on a stage, baring her soul, was a daunting prospect. But deep down, she knew she couldn't let her fear hold her back.

One evening, as Mia was practicing her acceptance speech in front of the mirror, her phone buzzed with a message. It was from Lily, a girl from her school who shared a similar reputation for shyness. They had never spoken much before, but Lily had also won an award at the same ceremony and wanted to reach out to her fellow awardee.

They met at a nearby café, two shy souls sitting in a quiet corner. As they exchanged stories about their creative pursuits, Mia realized that she wasn't alone in her apprehensions. Lily, too, had been terrified of the ceremony and the prospect of speaking publicly. Their shared experiences of shyness brought them closer together, and they decided to face their fears together.

Over the next few weeks, Mia and Lily met regularly to practice their speeches and offer each other support and encouragement. They discovered that their friendship not only helped them overcome their fears but also nurtured their creativity. They bounced ideas off each other, shared their work, and found inspiration in each other's words.

As the day of the awards ceremony approached, Mia and Lily's bond grew stronger. They had become each other's pillars of strength, and together they believed they could conquer their fears and shine on that stage. On the night of the event, they arrived early, their hearts pounding with anticipation.

As the ceremony began, Mia and Lily sat side by side in the front row, holding each other's hands for comfort. When it was Mia's turn to speak, she stepped onto the stage with Lily right behind her, offering a reassuring smile.

Mia took a deep breath, looked out at the audience, and began to speak.

Her voice was shaky at first, but as she delved into her story and shared her passion for writing, she felt a warmth spread through her. The audience listened intently, captivated by her words. Mia's confidence grew with each passing moment, and by the time she finished her speech, she had the entire room under her spell.

Lily was next, and Mia watched in awe as her friend confidently walked to the podium. Lily's speech was a testament to her own growth, and the audience gave her a standing ovation when she concluded. It was a night to remember, not only for Mia and Lily but for everyone in attendance.

The moment of truth came when the winners were announced. As Mia and Lily stood hand in hand, their hearts pounding, they heard their names called out one by one. Lily won second place, and Mia was declared the first-place winner. The audience erupted in applause as Mia walked up to receive her trophy, her heart brimming with gratitude.

In her acceptance speech, Mia spoke about the power of conquering shyness and the importance of nurturing creativity. She thanked Lily, her newfound friend, for helping her find the courage to face her fears. Mia's words resonated deeply with the audience, and they saw not just a talented young writer but also a brave, inspiring girl who had overcome her shyness to share her gift with the world.

The awards ceremony marked a turning point in Mia and Lily's lives. They continued to write and grow as writers, but they also became advocates for conquering shyness and nurturing creativity in others. They started a writing club at their school, where they encouraged their fellow students to express themselves through words and provided a supportive environment for budding writers.

Mia's talent for creative writing continued to shine, and as the years passed, her stories touched the hearts of readers far and wide. She knew that her gift was meant to be shared, and she had learned that facing her fears and finding a friend who understood her struggles had been the key to unlocking her true potential.

In the end, Mia and Lily's story was not just about the recognition of their writing talents but also about the power of friendship, the importance of conquering one's fears, and the positive outcomes that could stem from nurturing creativity. They had shown that with the right support and belief in oneself, even the shyest of individuals could find their voice and share their gifts with the world.

Camp Companions

Olivia had been counting down the days until summer camp for what felt like an eternity. She had heard all the exciting stories from her friends at school about the adventures awaiting her: fishing by the lake, camping under the starry night sky, canoeing down the winding river, and even trying her hand at archery. The prospect of endless outdoor activities had her buzzing with anticipation.

However, as the day of departure drew closer, Olivia's excitement began to mingle with a newfound apprehension. It wasn't the thought of braving the wilderness that made her anxious, but rather the idea of leaving home and spending time away from her family with a group of strangers. She'd heard tales of mischievous campers who played pranks on newcomers while they slept, and she couldn't help but wonder if she'd be their next target.

One evening, as Olivia sat on her bed, her older sister, Jessica, noticed the worry etched into her younger sibling's face. She sat down beside Olivia and asked, "What's on your mind, Liv? You've been a bundle of nerves lately."

Olivia hesitated for a moment, but she trusted her sister with her innermost thoughts. "I'm excited about camp, Jess, but I'm also scared. What if the girls in my cabin don't like me? What if they make fun of me? And what if they play pranks on me while I'm asleep?"

Jessica smiled warmly and put her arm around Olivia's shoulders. "I understand how you feel, Liv. It's normal to be nervous when you're about to meet new people and try new things. But you know what? Camp is also an incredible opportunity to make friends, have adventures, and grow as a person."

Olivia sighed, feeling a little reassured but still anxious. "I guess so, Jess, but it's just hard when you don't know anyone."

Jessica nodded thoughtfully. "I get it, but remember this: everyone else at camp will be in the same boat. They'll all be meeting new people, just like you. And you're a wonderful person, Liv. You're kind, friendly, and fun to be around. I have no doubt that you'll make friends in no time."

As the day of departure finally arrived, Olivia's anxiety bubbled within her like a pot of boiling water. Her parents drove her to the campgrounds, where she joined the bustling crowd of excited campers and their families.

Her heart raced as they approached the cabin area, and she spotted the rustic cabins nestled among the tall trees.

Once inside their cabin, Olivia met her bunkmates: Mia, Lily, and Emma. They were three girls around her age, and they seemed friendly enough. However, Olivia couldn't help but feel a twinge of anxiety gnawing at her as she unpacked her belongings and settled into her bunk.

The first day at camp was a whirlwind of activity. Olivia and her cabin mates participated in team-building exercises, enjoyed a picnic lunch by the lake, and even went fishing. Olivia was surprised to discover that she was quite skilled at casting her fishing line, and it earned her praise from her new friends.

As the days went by, Olivia gradually let her guard down. She and her cabin mates shared stories around the campfire, giggled in their bunks late at night, and formed a tight-knit group that looked out for each other. Olivia realized that they weren't the prank-pulling troublemakers she had feared; they were just girls like her, eager to make the most of their camp experience.

One evening, as they sat by the fire, Mia turned to Olivia and said, "You know, Liv, I was really nervous when I first got here, too. But now, I'm so glad we're friends."

Olivia smiled, her heart feeling light. "Me too, Mia. This has been so much fun."

The following week, the campers embarked on a two-day canoeing trip down the river. Olivia was a bit apprehensive about the journey, but she couldn't pass up the opportunity for adventure. With her cabin mates by her side, she paddled through calm waters and navigated tricky rapids, their laughter echoing through the river valley.

As they set up camp on the riverbank under the starlit sky, Lily pointed at the glittering constellations overhead. "Look at that, guys! It's like our own private planetarium."

Olivia gazed up at the stars, feeling grateful for the experiences she was sharing with her new friends. She realized that if she had let her initial anxiety hold her back, she would have missed out on all these incredible moments.

The last night of camp arrived all too soon. As the campers gathered around the campfire for one final evening, Olivia felt a bittersweet mix of emotions. She had gone from being a nervous newcomer to feeling like part of a close-knit family.

Jessica had been right all along, Olivia thought as she glanced at her cabin mates. Camp had been an opportunity to make new friends, embrace new experiences, and grow as a person. She had overcome her initial anxieties and come out of it with memories she would cherish forever.

As the campfire crackled and the stars twinkled overhead, Olivia made a silent promise to herself. She would never let fear or anxiety hold her back from trying new things or meeting new people. Camp had taught her that the world was full of opportunities and friends waiting to be discovered, even when it seemed daunting at first.

And so, as the campfire's warm glow enveloped her, Olivia knew that her summer camp experience had not only been about fishing, camping, canoeing, and archery. It had been about the journey of self-discovery, the joy of making new friends, and the realization that embracing new opportunities could lead to the most extraordinary adventures of all.

Julia and The Jealousy

Have you ever been jealous? Maybe your friend made another friend that they seemed to like more, or maybe you got a little sister that everyone seemed to love while you felt a little left behind? Maybe you were jealous because someone was better than you at something or because they got more attention than you?

Well, Julia felt jealous of the new girl in school, Susie. It can be difficult being jealous, and it can be hard knowing what to do.

You see, Julia did really well in school. She had lots of friends, she got good grades, and her teachers were always telling her how nice she was. Julia could count, she could write really neat letters, she could do a handstand and she had the longest hair out of everyone, and it didn't even get in the way in gym-class.

Julia was happy in school. That is, she was - until one day, the new girl started.

One morning, Miss Adams had a girl standing up by the black board with her. "This is Susie", said Miss Adams. "She's just moved here, and I want you all to be very nice and show her around and get her used to how everything is done, okay?"

Then, Miss Adams pulled a desk up right next to Julia's.

"This is Julia", she said. "She's going to be very helpful with getting to know the place, and she'll be well able to show you what's going on in class, okay?"

"Hi, I'm Susie!" the girl said and sat down next to Julia.

"Hi!" said Julia. "Don't worry, I'm going to show you everything."

As it turned out, it didn't seem like Susie needed a lot of help. Everytime Julia showed her something new in the books, Susie was already reading it. Everytime Julia tried showing her where to go in the hallways, someone else had already volunteered. When she tried to show her what to do in gym, she could do it already. She could do a handstand even faster than Julia, and when she did, it was clearly visible that her hair was even longer than Julia's and still didn't get in the way!

In the lunch queue, it seemed like everyone was walking up and asking if Susie wanted to come sit with them. The other kids were asking if she wanted to play with them during breaks, if she wanted to walk home with them, or if she wanted help with her homework.

The worst part was that Susie was so happy to answer everyone's questions, help them with their math and show them how to do handstands. How was she suddenly the go-to for those things? Julia started feeling a pang in her chest watching everyone crowd around Susie. She's not that great, she thought.

It got even worse. Julia started getting annoyed by what Susie was doing. She started saying things to her friends when Susie was out of earshot. "She walks like she has a bouncy-ball in her shoe." "She laughs too loud and it sounds weird." "She thinks she's so good at spelling, but she wrote 'halloe' instead of 'hollow' in class today!"

Julia started feeling like maybe she hated Susie. She hated how she always seemed to get what she wanted just because she was happy and smiling, and she hated how she always got to answer in the classroom when the teacher asked a question.

One day, Julia was hanging up her coat in her locker. Julia's best friend Laurie came up and took some books out.

"Hey, Laurie, do you want to come to my house today?" asked Julia.

"Oh… No thanks!" said Laurie. "I'm going to Susie's house after school."

Julia started boiling on the inside, and it felt like she couldn't breathe. First, Susie got to do all the stuff in class that Julia used to do, she got to have longer hair, then she got all the attention, and now, she was stealing Julia's best friend? It almost sounded like Lauri was trying to say something more, but Julia couldn't hear her because her face was so warm. She only nodded and went into class.

Susie was still sitting next to Julia. Julia hated it. She didn't answer any questions in class, and she didn't do her work properly because it would still never be as good as Susie's work, she thought. There was no point in anything; Julia wouldn't even be able to keep her friends. It was all unfair.

Then, Julia remembered she had a stick of gum in her desk. She wasn't allowed to have it, but she could probably sneak it into her mouth if she wanted. First, she thought, if she got caught chewing gum, she'd get in trouble and wouldn't have to sit next to Susie anymore that day. Then, she thought, if she put the gum on Susie's desk, maybe Susie would get in trouble and the teachers would like her less. Then, she had a really bad thought… What if she chewed the gum… and put it in Susie's hair..? What if she put the gum in Susie's long, stupid hair, and she'd have to cut it off?

Julia put the gum in her mouth and started chewing. Her cheeks were still warm and red all the way up to her eyes. She chewed the gum until it was the most sticky, and then, she spat it out into her hand. She checked that no one was looking, and quickly put it on the top of Susie's chair.

Susie moved back and forth a few times, and now, Julia started seeing it clearly in her head. Susie would lean back far enough, get the gum stuck, start touching it and get it stuck even more. Then, she'd ask Miss Adams what it was. Someone would see the gum, and they'd tell her there was no way to get it out without ripping or cutting hair off...

Julia started to feel bad. It really was awfully high up on the chair. Susie would have to cut so much. She would probably cry. She would be so sad about her hair. And it would all be Julia's fault...

Julia's heart started racing. Susie went to lean back...

"NO!" Julia screamed.

Susie jumped up. Everyone looked at them, and Miss Adams came rushing over.

"Is it a spider?!" cried Susie.

Everyone stared at Julia.

"No…" she said. "It's… there's gum, right there…"

Julia couldn't take it. She ran out. Miss Adams came and got her before she could run anywhere.

"Come here", Miss Adams said. She brought her into The Quiet Room. Susie was already sitting there. "Maybe you two have something you need to talk about?"

Julia was quiet for a long time.

"Thank you for saving my hair", Susie said.

Julia shook her head. "It was me who put the gum there", she said. "I… I feel like you're taking all my things, and taking my friends away, and I got mad, and… I'm sorry."

Julia started crying. Susie started crying, too. "I didn't want to take your friends away, I just wanted to be friends with you. You're so cool and you're good in school, and you showed me everything when I started. I've wanted you to be my friend ever since I got here."

"Really?" Julia asked.

"I have", Susie said. "Everyone else just lets me do things first or are nice to me because I'm new here, but you're actually showing me things the right way because it's the right way, and I want to do that, too. I was going to ask you to come to my house today with Laurie, because I thought, since she's your friend, she must be a good person too."

So that's what Laurie tried to say earlier, Julia thought. She was invited as well! Maybe Susie wasn't so bad. After all, Susie being better at math didn't make Julia bad at math, and Julia was better at spelling. She just couldn't see it before, because she was so jealous.

"I'm sorry I tried to put gum in your hair," she cried. "I got jealous because it was longer than mine."

"Really? I wish my hair was curly like yours, it's so pretty", Susie said.

Miss Adams was watching the girls make up with each other, and she was very proud. You see, it's not easy being jealous, but what you have to remember is that: everyone is special in their own way. Thinking about it differently makes it easier. Julia learned that you don't have to be the best at everything just to make people like you. All you have to do is be yourself, and that's enough.

If you're kind to people, and you do your best at your own pace, that's all that matters, because then, in no-time, you'll turn into the best "you" that there ever was - and who wouldn't want to be that?

Darla's Diary

Have you ever been afraid that your friends would do something that would hurt you, even though they were your friends? Maybe you've been worried that someone would find out a secret thought that you had, and then tell it to everyone?

Darla went through this, and it was very scary for her.

See, Darla got a diary for her birthday. It was a very nice looking book, where you could write your name on the outside, and it had a matching pen, eraser, and had dates on top of every page. Mom said it was a good thing to do, writing in a diary. "It helps organize your thoughts", said mom, "And if you have a problem, it will make you feel better. If you don't have anyone else to talk to, you can always talk to your diary."

At first, Darla thought it was kind of a silly thing of mom to say. How do you even talk to a book? Especially if you're only writing it for yourself! It started off a bit wobbly.

"Dear diary... I'm not used to this, but mom said I should try, so I'm going to. It's kinda' weird talking to a book... but I guess you're okay. Today I went to school and everything was okay. I had a dream about a rabbit. Mom made casserole with shrimp. Good night."

After a while, though, Darla felt like it was a lot easier to keep a diary. She would write down all sorts of thoughts and feelings in it, and the pages got longer and longer. Sometimes, she told it secrets. Sometimes, she wrote down her dreams. Sometimes, she wrote down things she would never ever want anyone to look at, and she was happy that she wouldn't have to show it to anyone - not even mom.

Darla started to bring her diary with her in her backpack when she was going away. It didn't feel right not to write in it before bedtime. When the pen was getting too short, she asked mom for a new one, and it was just as good of a pen, but it didn't match the diary anymore. It was okay though, and Darla told her diary all about it.

One day, something very scary happened. Darla was sure she had left her backpack in her locker, because she was going to have a sleep-over at her friend Carrie's house, so she had brought it with her in the morning. Only problem was, when she got to her locker, the backpack - and the diary - were gone!

"Oh no! Oh no, no, no!"

Darla started to panic. What if someone had gotten into her locker, taken her backpack, and was reading her diary? What if it was one of her friends, or one of the boys, or one of the teachers? What if it was someone who had taken her backpack and just left her diary on the school yard so that anyone could find it and see what she had written in it? What was she supposed to do? It would be the worst if the person who found it had told Mrs Gibbons how much she hated that she always smelled like old coffee grounds and made a horrible noise when she leaned over to help her in class, or if it was someone who would tell Howard that she liked him!

Anything that was in there would be so embarrassing if anyone found out. What if someone spread around that she was talking to herself on the toilet, or that every night before bed, she said goodnight to her pillow, like it was a person? If she went to the school reception, what if the receptionist had already taken it and read through it?

She was worried all day, and didn't know what to do. What do you do when something goes missing in school? Go to the police? The police would probably laugh at her, too. Darla thought for sure that her backpack was gone forever and all her secrets were going to be out. Then, in English class, she saw her friend Carrie wave to her from the other side of the room. She pointed down towards her feet, and there it was - her backpack! Carrie smiled, but Darla got so scared. Why did Carrie have her backpack? If she had the bag, she had definitely found the diary and read it.

Darla's stomach hurt when class was over and it was time to go home. She hurried over to Carrie.

"Darla, I found your bag outside, you must have left it by the benches before lunch. Good thing I was out late, huh?"

Darla was too anxious to be appreciative. She pulled the backpack out of Carrie's hands. "Did you take it out of my locker?!" ske asked.

Carrie looked confused. "No. I just found it. It was right outside."

Darla started walking out of school, going home instead of over to Carrie's house. Carrie ran after her.

"Hey! Darla, what's wrong?"

"You know what's wrong!" said Darla. "You know everything about everything now, so you can just tell everyone and laugh at me!"

Darla tried to walk away, but Carrie didn't let her go.

"I don't know what you're talking about", said Carrie, "Can you just stop running away for a second?"

Darla had tears in her eyes. "Now you know all about that I peeked over Jamie's shoulder on the test last week and how I slipped in the puddle yesterday and had to go back home and change my pants and how I like Howard and how I talk to myself like a crazy person, and you're just gonna tell everyone and laugh at me!"

Carrie stared at Darla. "What?" she said.

"You had my diary!"

Carrie laughed. "I know, but Darla… I didn't even look at it. I would never read your diary, it's private. You're my friend, I would never do that to you."

Carrie hugged Darla. Darla wiped a tear away.

"Besides", Carrie said, "Even if I had, I wouldn't say anything to anyone else. And just so you know, those things you just told me, they're not that weird. So you talk to yourself on the toilet - I talk to my dog! He doesn't know what I'm saying, but that doesn't stop me from telling him that I made a really bad fart in class and blamed Jamie for it!"

Both girls laughed.

"Do you still want to come to my house for a sleepover?" Carrie asked.

Darla nodded. Of course she wanted to go hang out with a good friend like Carrie.

Sometimes, we're afraid that people will judge us for the silliest reasons. Sure - some people do, and some people don't respect our privacy the way Carrie respected Darla - but those aren't people you want to be friends with. And just so you know, those "weird" things you do when no one is looking… We all do them, too!

Epilogue

Now that you've heard the stories of these amazing girls and the hurdles they've conquered, remember that you can do it too. You are an exceptional girl, and there is no one else in the world quite like you. Whenever you face fear, uncertainty, or doubt, take a deep breath and keep pushing forward. This is how you'll achieve remarkable things in the world.

Remember that it's okay to make mistakes; they are stepping stones on your journey to success. Learn from them and use them as opportunities to grow stronger and wiser. Surround yourself with positive influences and supportive friends who uplift and inspire you.

Believe in yourself, even when others may doubt you. Your potential is limitless, and your future is full of endless possibilities. With determination, resilience, and a positive attitude, you can overcome any obstacle and achieve greatness. Keep your head held high, young lady, for you are destined for incredible things."

Printed in Great Britain
by Amazon

55003156R00042